CONTENTS

WHAT IS A WOODLAND?

Woodlands are **habitats** with lots of trees. They look different in every **season**. They are warm in summer and cold in winter.

Pine, chestnut and oak trees grow in woodlands. Find out the name of the seed that grows on an oak tree.

chestnut tree

oak tree

pine tree

FACT CAT

WOODLAND

Izzi Howell

FACT CAT

Get your paws on this fantastic new mega-series from Wayland!

Join our Fact Cat on a journey of fun learning about every subject under the sun!

Published in paperback in 2016
First published in hardback in 2015
Copyright © Wayland 2015

Wayland, an imprint of Hachette Children's Group
Part of Hodder & Stoughton
Carmelite House
50 Victoria Embankment
London EC4Y 0DZ

ISBN: 978 0 7502 9473 7
ebook ISBN: 978 0 7502 9472 0
Dewey Number: 333.7'5-dc23
10 9 8 7 6 5 4 3 2 1

FSC
MIX
Paper from responsible sources
FSC® C104740

Editor: Izzi Howell
Design: Rocket Design (East Anglia) Ltd
Fact Cat illustrations: Shutterstock/Julien Troneur
Other illustrations: Stefan Chabluk
Consultant: Kate Ruttle

Produced for Wayland by
White-Thomson Publishing Ltd
www.wtpub.co.uk
+44 (0) 843 208 7460

An Hachette UK Company
www.hachette.co.uk
www.hachettechildrens.co.uk

Printed and bound in China

Picture and illustration credits:
Dreamstime: Waclaw Bugno 4, Angelo Gilardelli 4, Rangizzz 14, Mtilghma 18; Shutterstock: Volodymyr Burdiak cover, Piotr Krzeslak 4, 3523studio 4, S.Borisov 6, Masalski Maksim 7, Vishnevskiy Vasily 8, Vitaly Ilyasov 9, FomaA 10, Ron Rowan Photography 11, Gleb Tarro 11, Matt Gore 12, Chantal de Bruijne 13, Mickael BUONO 14, neil hardwick 14, Dariush M 14, mlorenz 15, Catalin Petolea 16, Vlad Siaber 16, Henk Jacobs 17, Jiri Hera 17, Pavelk 19, Brian Balster 20, BMJ 21; Stefan Chabluk: 5, Thinkstock: Brian Swartz title page, soleg 7, stanzi11 10

Every effort has been made to clear copyright. Should there be any inadvertent omission, please apply to the publisher for rectification.

The author, Izzi Howell, is a writer and editor specialising in children's educational publishing.

The consultant, Kate Ruttle, is a literacy expert and SENCO, and teaches in Suffolk.

FACT CAT FACT

There is a question for you to answer on each spread in this book. You can check your answers on page 24.

There are woodlands all over the world, in places such as North America, Europe and Asia. The biggest woodland area in the world covers the north of Europe and Russia.

Some woodland animals, such as owls, live all over the world. Other woodland animals, such as raccoons, only live in North America.

North America

Europe

Asia

Africa

South America

Australia

▨ Woodland

FACT CAT FACT

The tallest trees in the world are found in the woodlands of California, in the USA. These giant redwood trees are up to 115 metres tall, which is the same as 23 giraffes standing on top of each other!

TYPES OF TREE

There are two types of woodland tree: **deciduous** and **evergreen**. The leaves of deciduous trees change colour in autumn. They go from green to red, orange or yellow.

In winter, deciduous trees, such as oak trees, lose all their leaves. Their leaves will grow back in spring. Every year, each oak tree grows and loses about 250,000 leaves.

The leaves of evergreen trees, such as pine trees, look the same in every season. They stay green all year round.

People often use evergreen leaves and pine cones to decorate their homes in winter.

ring

FACT CAT FACT

We can find out the age of a tree by counting the rings inside its **trunk**. A new ring grows every year. Find out the age of the oldest living tree in the world.

CHANGING SEASONS

The woodland is full of life in spring and summer. New leaves and flowers grow on plants and deciduous trees. Lots of animals have new **young** to look after.

Young birds live in a **nest**. Other young animals live in **burrows** or holes in trees.

FACT CAT FACT

We sometimes use different names for very young animals. Young foxes are called cubs. A young rabbit is called a kitten. Find out the name for a young deer.

In autumn, the woodland is full of food for animals. Some animals **bury** extra food in the ground to eat during winter, when there is less food available.

Some animals, such as this hedgehog, **hibernate** in winter. This means that they go to sleep at the beginning of winter. They wake up in spring when it is warmer.

WILDLIFE

Brown is a good colour for **camouflage** in the woodland. Deer and moose have brown **fur** so that other animals can't see them easily.

We know that this is a male deer because it has **antlers**.

antlers

This woodpecker eats insects that live inside trees. It has a strong beak that can make holes in trees to find insects.

It's hard to see far in the woodland because there are lots of trees, so woodland animals also use their noses to find food.

This grizzly bear is looking for food with her cubs. Find out what grizzly bears eat.

FACT CAT FACT

Grizzly bears can smell other animals from 30 kilometres away.

Chipmunks carry food back to their homes in their cheeks. Their cheeks can grow up to three times the size of their head!

PLANTS

In some woodlands, the ground is covered by bluebells in spring. This is called a bluebell carpet, because it looks like a floor made of flowers!

Ferns are one of the oldest woodland plants. They have been on Earth for millions of years. We think that some dinosaurs used to eat ferns.

bluebells

fern

Mushrooms get their food from dead plants or animals. You can often find mushrooms growing on dead logs or **tree stumps**.

This mushroom is very dangerous to touch. It is **poisonous**. Find out why poisonous plants are often brightly coloured.

FACT CAT FACT

Giant puffball mushrooms can grow to more than one metre wide. They are so big that some people think they are sheep from far away!

A FOOD CHAIN

Woodland animals and plants get all their food from their habitat. Plants make their own food with the help of sunlight. Woodland animals eat plants or other animals.

Sunlight (makes food for)

Clover (eaten by)

We can use a food chain to see where animals and plants get their food from. Find out the word for animals, such as voles, that only eat plants.

Tawny owl

Vole (eaten by)

Food chains show us how everything is connected in woodlands. For example, tawny owls don't eat plants, but plants are still important to them. This is because tawny owls eat voles who need plants to survive.

Moose eat up to 32 kg of plants every day!

The "too-wit-too-woo" noise that tawny owls make at night is actually two owls calling to each other. The female owl calls, "too-wit" and the male owl answers, "too-woo"!

FOOD FROM THE WOODS

Lots of tasty things grow in the woodland, but you should never eat any woodland plants without asking an adult first. You have probably eaten blackberries, but have you tried cooked stinging nettles? They taste like spinach!

Plants in the woodland have special ways to stop us eating them. Blackberry plants have sharp **thorns**. Nettles will **sting** you if you touch them, so this person is wearing gloves.

blackberry

nettle

Maple syrup comes from a woodland tree. If you make a hole in a maple tree in spring, maple syrup will come out. Find out which breakfast food is often eaten with maple syrup.

Canada produces most of the world's maple syrup. Every year, they make over 26 million litres, which is enough to fill nearly 200,000 bathtubs.

Raw maple syrup has a light colour. Before it is put in bottles, it is heated. This makes it turn darker.

VISITING WOODLANDS

Lots of woodlands are part of national parks. A national park is an area that is **protected**.

This black bear lives in Yellowstone National Park in the USA. Yellowstone became the first national park in the world nearly 150 years ago.

FACT CAT FACT

Under the woodlands in Yellowstone National Park is a huge underground volcano. The volcano is active, so it might **erupt** one day!

Many woodlands and national parks have special **trails** where people can walk. Trails mean that people can visit the woodland without **damaging** the habitat.

Sherwood Forest, in the UK, has lots of trails to explore. Find out which famous stories take place in Sherwood Forest.

PROTECTING WOODLANDS

All over the world, people cut down woodlands. They use the wood and build houses. Lots of animals and plants are losing their habitats.

When animals lose their habitat, they can become **endangered**. Find out two endangered woodland animals.

It is important to protect the woodlands by making them into national parks. We can also plant trees, which will grow into new woodlands.

In some countries, people are helping endangered animals to come back to the woodlands. Scientists have brought a group of beavers from Norway to live in Scotland. Beavers haven't lived in Scotland for 400 years, but now they live there again.

FACT CAT FACT

Beavers have see-through **eyelids** that they use for swimming under water. They are like goggles to stop water getting in their eyes.

QUIZ Try to answer the questions below. Look back through the book to help you. Check your answers on page 24.

1 It is always hot in the woodlands. True or not true?

a) true
b) not true

2 Deciduous trees lose their leaves in winter. True or not true?

a) true
b) not true

3 Blue is a good colour for camouflage in the woodland. True or not true?

a) true
b) not true

4 Mushrooms get their food from dead plants or animals. True or not true?

a) true
b) not true

5 Most of the world's maple syrup comes from Canada. True or not true?

a) true
b) not true

6 It isn't important to protect woodlands. True or not true?

a) true
b) not true

GLOSSARY

antlers large horns that grow on the heads of male deer

burrow a hole in the ground that animals such as foxes and badgers live in

bury to put something in a hole in the ground and cover it

camouflage hiding by making yourself the same colour as the area you are in

damage to hurt something

deciduous a type of tree whose leaves change colour and fall off in winter

endangered an animal or plant is endangered when there are only very few of its kind left in the world

erupt when smoke and lava come out of a volcano

evergreen a type of tree that doesn't lose its leaves in winter

eyelid what stops you seeing when you close your eye

fur the hair of an animal

habitat the area where a plant or an animal lives

hibernate to sleep all winter and wake up in spring

nest a place where birds lay eggs and feed their young

poisonous describes something that can hurt or kill you if you touch it or eat it

protect to keep something safe

raw uncooked

season different parts of the year called spring, summer, autumn and winter

sting to prick your skin and hurt you

thorns sharp parts of a plant that will hurt you if you touch them

trail a path made for hiking

tree stump the short part of the tree that is left when you cut it down

trunk the main stem of a tree, apart from the branches and leaves

young an animal's babies

INDEX

ANSWERS

Pages 4–20

Page 4: an acorn

Page 7: over 5,000 years old

Page 8: a fawn

Page 11: plants such as berries, and animals such as moose, salmon and bison

Page 13: to show other animals not to eat them

Page 14: herbivore

Page 17: pancakes or French toast

Page 19: the stories of Robin Hood

Page 20: endangered woodland animals include bears, wolves, caribou and many species of bat

Quiz answers

1 not true, it depends on the season

2 true

3 not true, brown is much better

4 true

5 true

6 not true, it is very important!